TWELVE
CATS
FOR CHRISTMAS
MARTIN LEMAN

First published 1982 by
Pelham Books Ltd

Picturemac edition published 1988 by
Macmillan Children's Books
A division of Macmillan Publishers Limited
London and Basingstoke
Associated companies throughout the world

Reprinted 1989

British Library Cataloguing in Publication Data
Leman Martin
    Twelve cats for Christmas
    I. Title
    823'.914[J]

ISBN 0-333-48083-X

Printed in Hong Kong

TWELVE CATS
FOR CHRISTMAS
MARTIN LEMAN

M

MACMILLAN CHILDREN'S BOOKS

On the first day of Christmas
my true love gave to me
**a black cat
in a pear tree**

On the second day of Christmas
my true love gave to me

a stripy ginger
kitten

and a black cat in a pear tree

On the third day of Christmas
my true love gave to me
a moonlit cat
smiling
a stripy ginger kitten
and a black cat in a pear tree

On the fourth day of Christmas
my true love gave to me

an amber cat
resting

a moonlit cat smiling
a stripy ginger kitten
and a black cat in a pear tree

On the fifth day of Christmas
my true love gave to me

a fat little tabby

an amber cat resting
a moonlit cat smiling
a stripy ginger kitten
and a black cat in a pear tree

On the sixth day of Christmas
my true love gave to me

a white cat
waiting

a fat little tabby
an amber cat resting
a moonlit cat smiling
a stripy ginger kitten
and a black cat in a pear tree

On the seventh day of Christmas
my true love gave to me

a seaside cat
purring

a white cat waiting
a fat little tabby
an amber cat resting
a moonlit cat smiling
a stripy ginger kitten
and a black cat in a pear tree

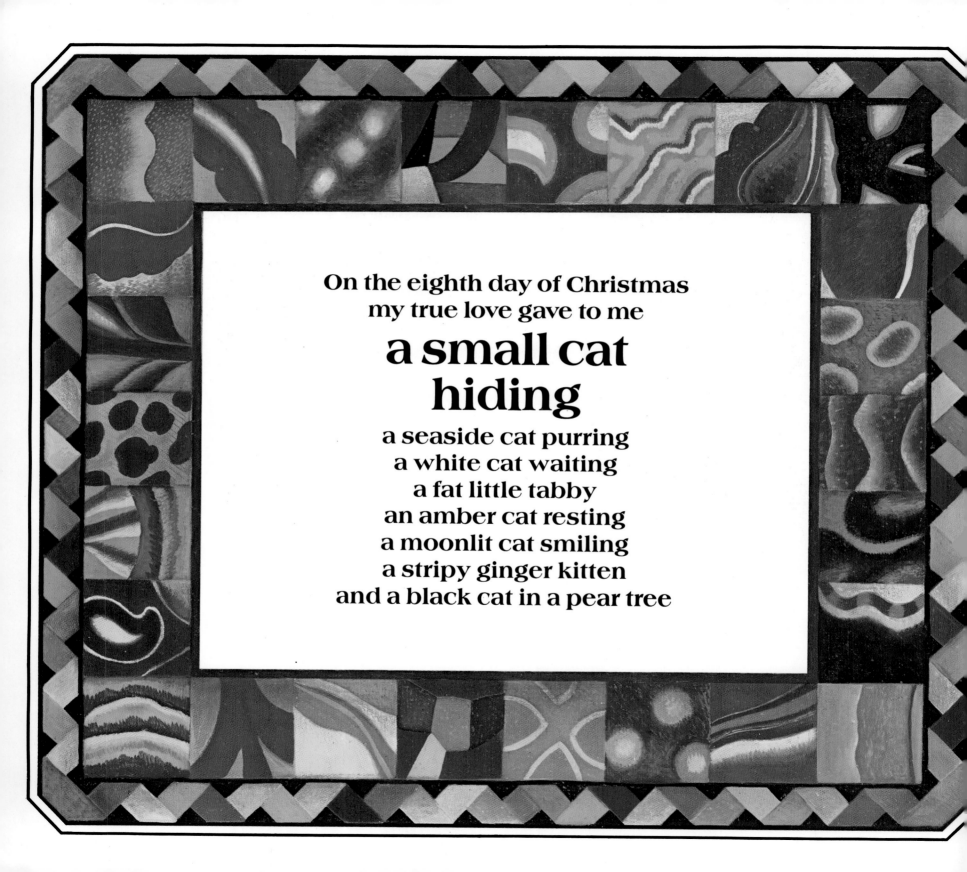

On the eighth day of Christmas
my true love gave to me

a small cat
hiding

a seaside cat purring
a white cat waiting
a fat little tabby
an amber cat resting
a moonlit cat smiling
a stripy ginger kitten
and a black cat in a pear tree

On the ninth day of Christmas
my true love gave to me

a naughty cat playing

a small cat hiding
a seaside cat purring
a white cat waiting
a fat little tabby
an amber cat resting
a moonlit cat smiling
a stripy ginger kitten
and a black cat in a pear tree

On the tenth day of Christmas
my true love gave to me

a grey cat walking

a naughty cat playing
a small cat hiding
a seaside cat purring
a white cat waiting
a fat little tabby
an amber cat resting
a moonlit cat smiling
a stripy ginger kitten
and a black cat in a pear tree

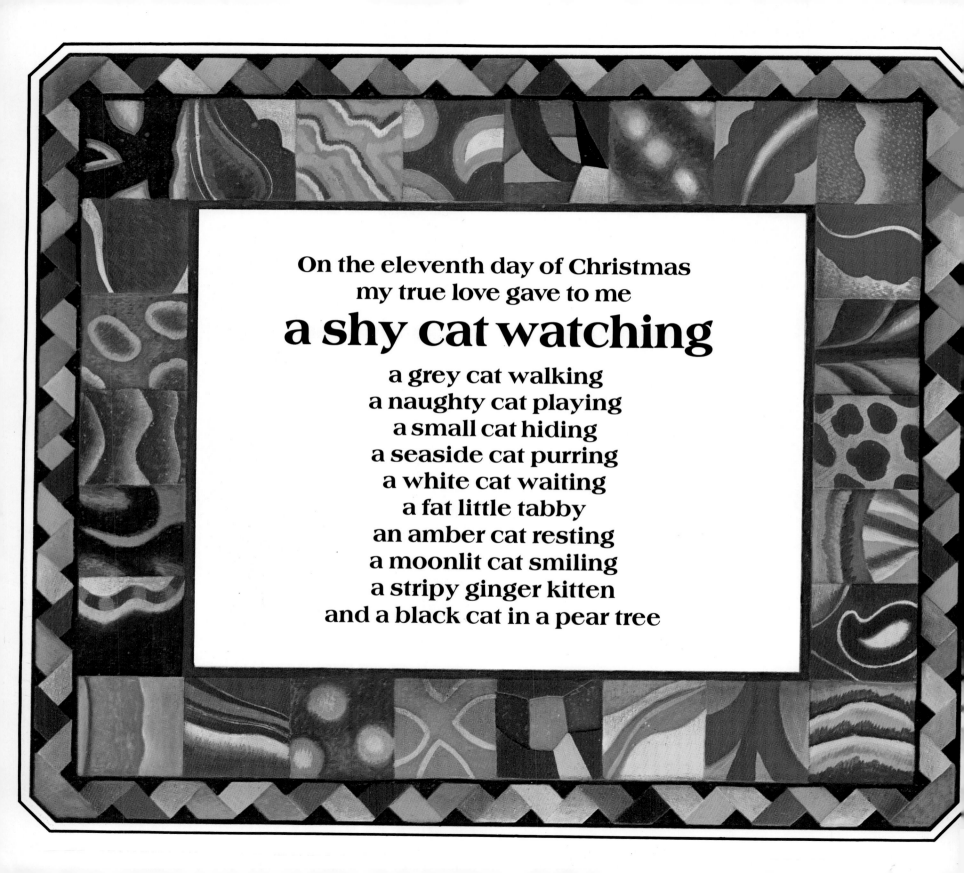

On the eleventh day of Christmas
my true love gave to me

a shy cat watching

a grey cat walking
a naughty cat playing
a small cat hiding
a seaside cat purring
a white cat waiting
a fat little tabby
an amber cat resting
a moonlit cat smiling
a stripy ginger kitten
and a black cat in a pear tree

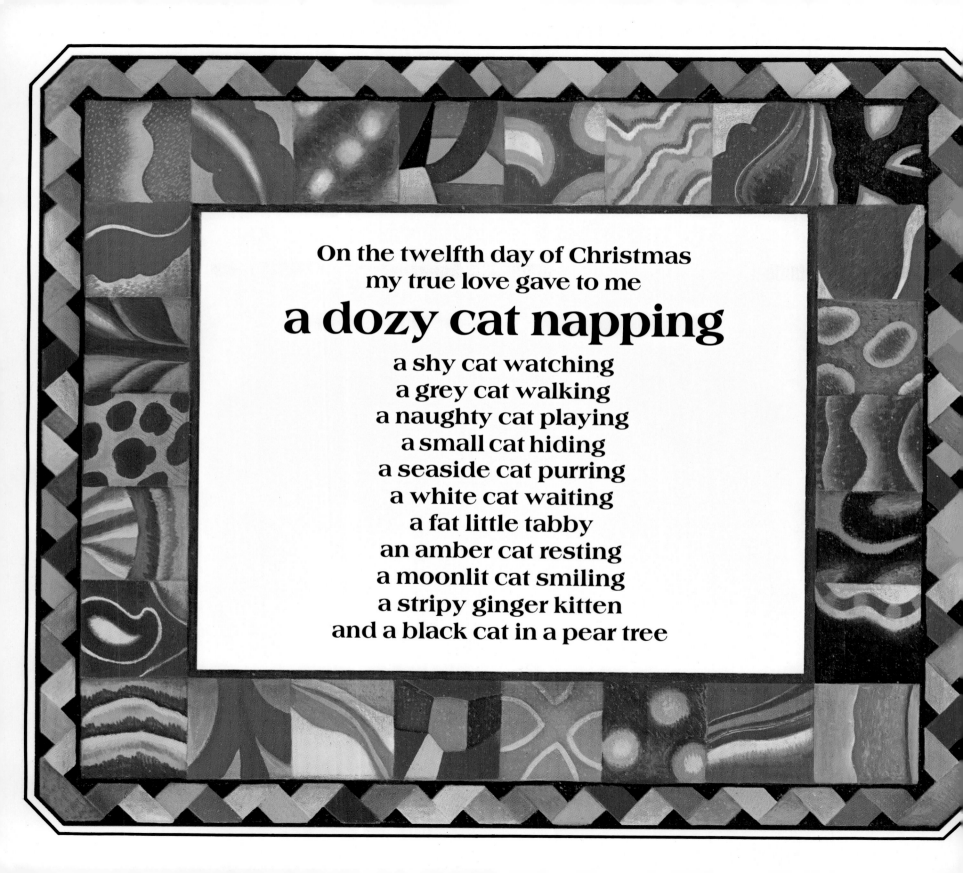

On the twelfth day of Christmas
my true love gave to me

a dozy cat napping

a shy cat watching
a grey cat walking
a naughty cat playing
a small cat hiding
a seaside cat purring
a white cat waiting
a fat little tabby
an amber cat resting
a moonlit cat smiling
a stripy ginger kitten
and a black cat in a pear tree

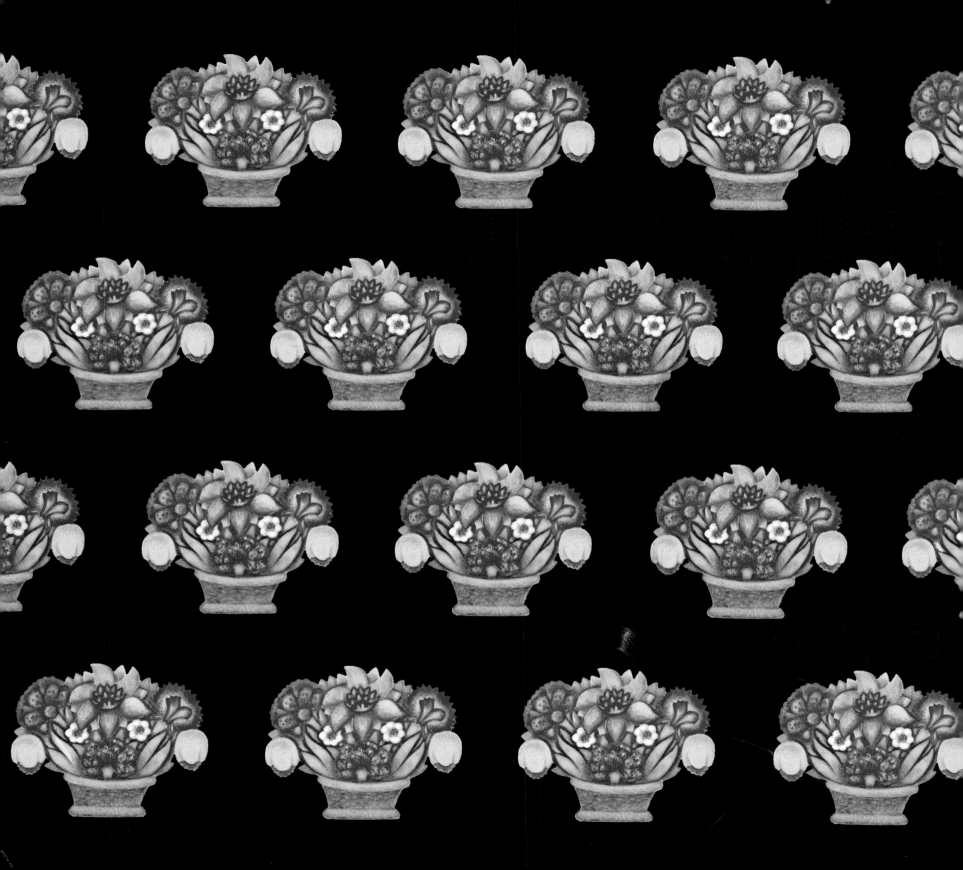

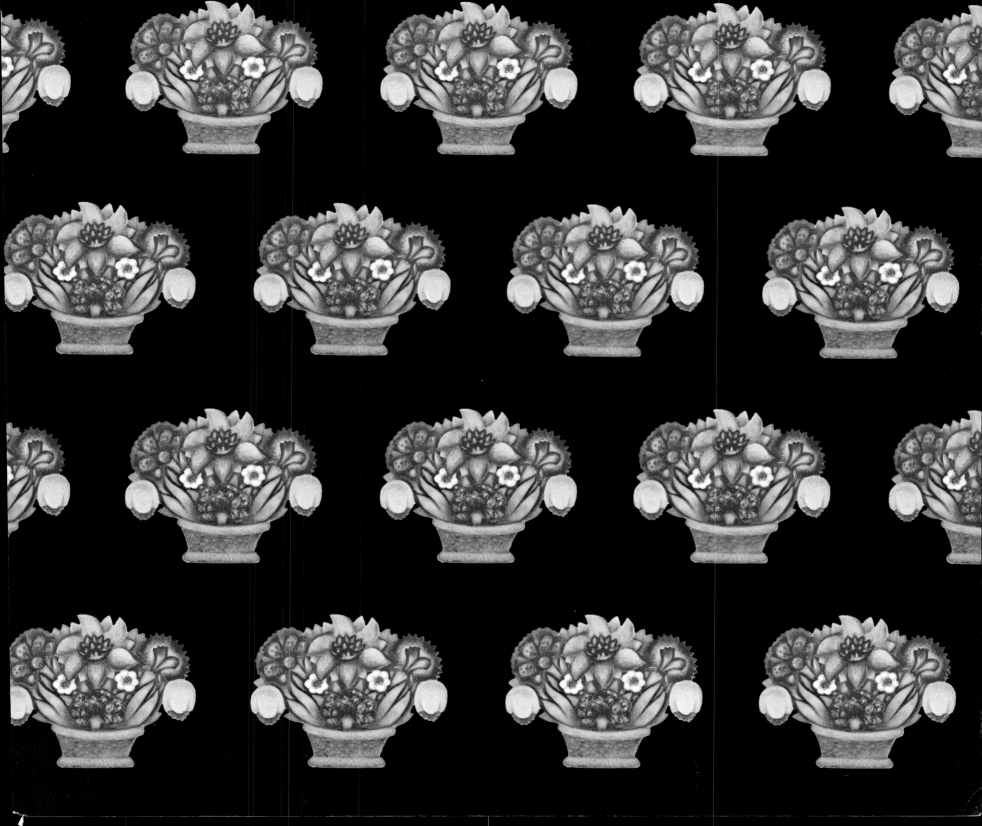

Other Picturemacs you will enjoy

BRINGING THE RAIN TO KAPITI PLAIN Verna Aardema/Beatriz Vidal
BIMWILI & THE ZIMWI Verna Aardema/Susan Meddaugh
OH, KOJO! HOW COULD YOU! Verna Aardema/Marc Brown
THE KING'S FLOWER Mitsumasa Anno
THROUGH THE MAGIC MIRROR Anthony Browne
NUNGU AND THE CROCODILE Babette Cole
TRICK A TRACKER Michael Foreman
I'LL TAKE YOU TO MRS COLE! Nigel Gray/Michael Foreman
AESOP'S FABLES Heidi Holder
THE TRIP TO PANAMA Janosch
THE MICE NEXT DOOR Anthony Knowles/Susan Edwards
JELLY BELLY Dennis Lee/Juan Wijngaard
FABLES Arnold Lobel
MAGICAL CHANGES Graham Oakley
HENRIETTA GOOSE Abigail Pizer
ALISTAIR'S TIME MACHINE Marilyn Sadler/Roger Bollen
IMOGENE'S ANTLERS David Small
WOLF'S FAVOUR Fulvio Testa
CURTIS THE HIP-HOP CAT Gini Wade
SIXES AND SEVENS John Yeoman/Quentin Blake
THE BEAR'S WINTER HOUSE John Yeoman/Quentin Blake
THE BEAR'S WATER PICNIC John Yeoman/Quentin Blake
BEATRICE AND VANESSA John Yeoman/Quentin Blake

For a complete list of Picturemac titles write to:

Macmillan Children's Books, 18–21 Cavaye Place, London SW10 9PG